SCHOLASTIC
News
Nonfiction Readers

Dinosaur Teeth

by Susan H. Gray

Children's Press®
A Division of Scholastic Inc.
New York Toronto London Auckland Sydney
Mexico City New Delhi Hong Kong
Danbury, Connecticut

These content vocabulary word builders are for grades 1–2.

Subject Consultant: Rudyard W. Sadleir, Doctoral Candidate in Evolutionary Biology, University of Chicago, Chicago, Illinois

Reading Consultant: Cecilia Minden-Cupp, PhD, Former Director of the Language and Literacy Program, Harvard Graduate School of Education, Cambridge, Massachusetts

Photographs © 2007: Alamy Images: 23 bottom left (Phil Degginger/Carnegie Museum), back cover, 23 top right (Russ Merne); Corbis Images: cover (Layne Kennedy), 19 (Richard T. Nowitz), 5 bottom right, 16 (Anthony John West); Getty Images: 23 bottom right (Vanderlei Almedia/AFP), 20 top (Louie Psihoyos/Science Faction); JupiterImages/ Oxford Scientific/Highlights for Children: 1, 4 top, 11; Natural History Museum, London: 5 bottom left, 12 (John Holmes), 4 bottom right, 9 (John Sibbick), 2, 23 top left; Photo Researchers, NY: 4 bottom left, 5 top left, 7 (Carlos Goldin), 20 bottom (Stephen J. Krasemann), 17 (Tom McHugh), 5 top right, 15 (Laurie O'Keefe), 13 (Joe Tucciarone); The Field Museum, Chicago, IL: 21 bottom (GEO86246_6c, photographer John Weinstein).
Illustration by James E. Whitcraft

Book Design: Simonsays Design!
Book Production: The Design Lab

Library of Congress Cataloging-in-Publication Data
Gray, Susan Heinrichs.
  Dinosaur teeth / by Susan H. Gray.
     p. cm. — (Scholastic news nonfiction readers)
  Includes bibliographical references and index.
  ISBN-13: 978-0-531-17484-5
  ISBN-10: 0-531-17484-0
  1. Teeth, Fossil—Juvenile literature. 2. Dinosaurs—Juvenile literature. I. Title. II. Series.
  QE846G73 2007
  567.9—dc22   2006024054

1 2 3 4 5 6 7 8 9 10 R 16 15 14 13 12 11 10 09 08 07

CONTENTS

WORD HUNT

Look for these words as you read. They will be in **bold**.

carnivores
(**kar**-nih-vorz)

paleontologists
(pale-ee-uhn-
tol-uh-jists)

predator
(**pred**-uh-tur)

4

fossils
(**foss**-uhlz)

herbivores
(**ur**-bih-vorz)

prey
(pray)

shrubs
(shruhbz)

TEETH EVERYWHERE

Dinosaur teeth have been found in many places around the world. **Paleontologists**, scientists who study **fossils**, have found thousands of them. Fossils are the remains of plants and animals from millions of years ago.

A paleontologist looks at the fossil teeth on a jawbone in South America.

Teeth can tell us a lot about dinosaurs.

They tell us whether a dinosaur was a plant eater or a fierce **predator** that ate meat.

They can also tell us whether a dinosaur chewed its food or gulped its food down whole.

Predators are animals that hunt other animals for food.

Animals that eat meat are called **carnivores**.

Meat-eating dinosaurs had large, sharp teeth. Many had curved teeth with notched edges.

These dinosaur carnivores used their teeth to slice flesh and hold on to a struggling animal.

Allosaurus was a large carnivore.

Some dinosaurs had long, narrow jaws like the jaws of some crocodiles.

Scientists think these dinosaurs probably hunted and ate fish. Their teeth were great for clamping down on **prey**.

prey

Spinosaurus hunts for fish in shallow water.

Animals that eat plants are called **herbivores**. Some dinosaur herbivores had hundreds of teeth!

These dinosaurs had rows and rows of teeth. They used their teeth to cut up pieces of plants.

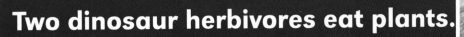
Two dinosaur herbivores eat plants.

15

Some dinosaurs had no front teeth at all. Instead, they had hard beaks.

They used their beaks to rip plants from the ground. They also used them to tear branches from **shrubs**. They cut everything up with their side teeth.

shrubs

Triceratops used its beak to pull plants out of the ground.

The dinosaurs' teeth were always wearing down or falling out. But new ones kept growing in.

Some dinosaurs went through more than a thousand teeth in their lives!

Today, paleontologists find some of those teeth as fossils. Maybe someday you will find one, too!

A scientist removes a dinosaur tooth fossil from the ground.

TOOTHY TALES

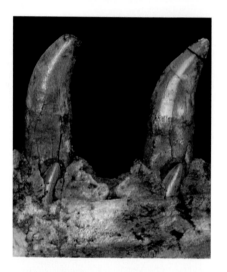

These dinosaur teeth were light in color when the dinosaur was alive. After the dinosaur died, its teeth turned dark as they became fossils.

This dinosaur probably had more teeth when it died. But those teeth were lost over millions of years.

This bone has tooth marks in it. The dinosaur that owned it probably became another dinosaur's meal!

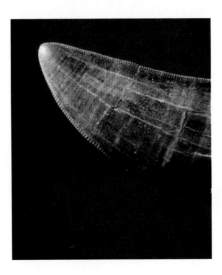

This dinosaur tooth was found with no skeleton or skull nearby. It might have pulled loose as the dinosaur ate a tough meal.

YOUR NEW WORDS

carnivores (**kar**-nih-vorz) animals that eat meat

fossils (**foss**-uhlz) remains of plants or animals from millions of years ago

herbivores (**ur**-bih-vorz) animals that eat plants

paleontologists (pale-ee-uhn-**tol**-uh-jists) scientists who study fossils to learn about animals and plants that lived millions of years ago

predator (**pred**-uh-tur) an animal that hunts other animals for food

prey (pray) an animal that is hunted for food

shrubs (shruhbz) short, woody bushes

CARNIVORE OR HERBIVORE?

herbivore

carnivore

herbivore

carnivore

INDEX

FIND OUT MORE
Book:
Mattern, Joanne. *Dinosaur Teeth and Beaks.* Milwaukee: Weekly Reader Early Learning Library, 2005.

Website:
ZoomDinosaurs.com
www.enchantedlearning.com/subjects/dinosaurs

MEET THE AUTHOR
Susan H. Gray has a master's degree in zoology. She has written more than seventy science and reference books for children. She especially loves to write about animals. Susan and her husband, Michael, live in Cabot, Arkansas.